Guinea Beginner's Guide Ownership & Care

Jennifer Grewer

© 2015

ISBN-13: 978-1517345631

ISBN-10: 1517345634

DISCLAIMER

All rights reserved. No part of this publication may be reproduced, distributed, or transmitted in any form or by any means, including photocopying, recording, or other electronic or mechanical methods, without the prior written permission of the publisher, except in the case of brief quotations embodied in critical reviews and certain other non-commercial uses permitted by copyright law.

Although the author and publisher have made every effort to ensure that the information in this book was correct at press time, the author and publisher do not assume and hereby disclaim any liability to any party for any loss, damage, or disruption caused by errors or omissions, whether such errors or omissions result from negligence, accident, or any other cause.

Cover Photo: "Guinea-pig-booboo-lieveheersbeestje-14" by Guinea pig - Own work. Licensed under CC BY-SA 4.0 via Wikimedia Commons - https://commons.wikimedia.org/wiki/File:Guinea-pig-booboo-lieveheersbeestje-14.jpg#/media/File:Guinea-pig-booboo-lieveheersbeestje-14.jpg (Uploaded by Hayvan Uzmani). Image has been cropped & text added. Thank you photographer for releasing under CC license.

Table of Contents

Introduction 3

Chapter 1: Origin of the Breed 5

   Types of Guinea Pigs 7

   Guinea Pig Behavior 11

   Difference between a Guinea Pig and a Hamster 15

Chapter 2: Cost of Owning a Guinea Pig 18

Chapter 3: Bringing Home a Guinea Pig 20

   Choosing a Guinea Pig 20

   Guinea pig Buying Tips 23

Chapter 4: Guinea Pig Care 25

   Housing for Guinea Pigs 25

   Feeding your Guinea Pigs 29

   Veterinary Care for Guinea Pigs 32

   Training a Guinea Pig 33

Chapter 5: Showing a Guinea Pig 36

   Introduction to showing guinea pigs 36

   Grooming a Guinea Pig 37

Chapter 6: Pregnancy and Birth 40

   Mating Behavior 40

   Pregnancy 41

   The Babies 41

Conclusion 43

Introduction

Bringing a pet home requires a great deal of preparation. It is important to understand which pet suits the mentality and the habits of all the members of a household. So, there is a lot of research that is required when you are bringing home a pet such as a cat or a dog. But, many people like to bring home the cute little rotund rodents, guinea pigs assuming that they need nothing more than a cage and some food and water. Well, the truth is that when you are bringing home a guinea pig, there is just as much prep that is required.

Often brought home on an impulse, guinea pigs and other rodents such as hamsters usually find themselves in rather hostile households. While you may try your best to take good care of your furry little friend, there could be several important things that you are missing out or even neglecting. That is why, you need a guide or a set of instructions that can help you take better care of this new member of your family. Even though the guinea pig seems like an ideal pet for a child, you need to ensure that you take enough care of the little creature. In fact, there are far more minute details that you need to keep in mind when you are taking care of an animal as little as the guinea pig. They are more prone to hazards, diseases and even injuries if they are not maintained under good conditions.

The reason why these animals are brought home is their gentle demeanour. They cannot cause any harm and of course, they are extremely adorable creatures. Even if they bite, as they will at times, it will be more of a gentle nibble rather than a painful dig. They are ideal for homes with young children as they make great companions and can also be used to teach children important lessons about responsibility.

This book is primarily aimed at becoming the manual that you need to take good care of your guinea pig. It covers all the common questions that first-time guinea pig owners could possibly have. The history and origin of the breed, the types of guinea pigs that you can choose from, the right food and the proper housing necessary for these cute creatures are some of the topics that are covered in this book.

If you are interested in showing your guinea pigs, the guidelines and the right way of showing your guinea pig are topics that might be of great interest to you. You will also learn to groom your pet correctly. The exercises that you need to keep your pet healthy are also covered in this book. One important fact that is covered in this book is the difference between hamsters and guinea pigs. Most pet owners are unaware of this difference which makes them apply wrong methods of grooming and caring for their pets.

You will know if the guinea pig is the right pet for you by the time you are done reading this book. If you are convinced that you can bring home a guinea pig and take good care of it, then I will consider the purpose of this guide fulfilled.

Chapter 1: Origin of the Breed

Also known as "cavies", guinea pigs have been domesticated for several years now. They are found in the wild in South America where they inhabit the edges of forests, rocky regions and also grasslands. These animals are usually found in groups of 10 and make their homes in burrows. They are nocturnal creatures that come out at nights to look for food to eat. But the main question here is when did they first get domesticated?

They were domesticated as early as 5000 BC. Mostly used for food, these creatures were domesticated by tribes in the Andean region. Several excavations in these regions of South America gave revealed statuettes that represented the guinea pig. Most excavations were conducted in Ecuador and Peru. It is believed that the Moche people who lived in Peru worshipped the guinea pig and hence gave it a special place in their art. Even today, these animals are an important source of food in the Andean highlands where they are raised on vegetable scraps produced by the families.

Several breeds of the guinea pig sprung up from 1200 AD to 1532. These breeds are the ancestors of the guinea pigs as we know them today. There are several traditions and folklore that involve guinea pigs. Historians reveal that these animals were exchanged as gifts. They also formed an important part of several rituals and traditional celebrations.

Several traditional healing rituals, also known as curanderos include guinea pigs as a major part of the rituals. Folk doctors believed that the animals could diagnose diseases like typhus, arthritis, jaundice and arthritis. It was believed that the guinea pigs are a supernatural medium. They were rubbed against the bodies of people who were ill in order to diagnose these conditions. The black guinea pigs, in particular, were considered to be useful in diagnosing diseases. Sometimes, these rituals would take an ugly turn where the entrails of the animal were removed to see if the cure had worked. Perhaps, that is how the popular saying about "being a guinea pig" to experiments came into existence. Even today, in several regions of the Andes, these methods are still practiced. These people are not very fond of Western medicine and tend to stick to their traditional ways.

Guinea pigs were first brought to Europe by the English, Spanish and Dutch traders. Very quickly, they became extremely popular as exotic pets. Initially, they were only domesticated by the royalty and the rich. It is said that even Queen Elizabeth had guinea pigs for pets.

A description of this creature for Santo Domingo that was written in 1547 is considered the earliest record of the creature available. Also, since the guinea pig is not a native of Spain, it was concluded that they were introduced in this area by the traders.

According to excavations that were conducted in the West Indies, it is indicated that the animals were introduced by horticulturists from South America who also made ceramics. This was as early as 500 BC when the guinea pigs were brought from South America to the Caribbean Island.

These rodents were also seen in Puerto Rico before the Spaniards invaded the region. An accurate and scientific description of the creature was written in the West in the year 1554 by Conard Gessner who was a Swedish naturalist. The binomial name was given by Erxleben in the year 1777.

An illustration of the guinea pig that is on display in the National Portrait Gallery in London is believed to be the earliest one of the creature. It was made in the year 1580 and shows a little girl donning an Elizabethan dress. She is seen holding a guinea pig in her hands while her brothers watch holding their pet bird. The estimated date of this picture is the same as the earliest found remains of the guinea pig in England. A partial skeleton of the guinea pig was found in a manor house in Essex in around 1575.

Since then, the guinea pig has grown in popularity as a great pet. The docile creature is one the most preferred species in homes with children in particular. Of course, there are several types of guinea pigs to choose from today. We will discuss the types of cavies in detail in the next section of this chapter.

Types of Guinea Pigs

When you have decided to bring home the guinea pig, you would be surprised to find that there are so many varieties of this rodent that you can choose from. Below is a list of most commonly found guinea pigs. They are mostly classified on the basis of their appearance. Guinea pigs are very distinct with respect to the type of fur that you will find on their body. The color, the texture and even the length of the hair varies, giving you several pretty pets to choose from. Think of the grooming needs when you pick a breed to bring home.

Abyssinian Guinea Pig

This type of guinea pig comes in a variety of colors. The most distinct characteristic of this breed is that the fur consists of tall and round swirls of hair across the body. They are also found in the satin variety if you want one.

American Guinea Pig

This is perhaps the most common type of guinea pig that you will see. Actually the image of the guinea pig that most people have in their minds is perhaps that of the American Guinea Pig. The hair of the American Guinea is short and smooth. The body is rotund and chubby. This breed is also available in the satin variety. There is a range of colors that you can choose from in this breed. The most distinctive feature of this breed is its demeanour. It is considered to be the calmest variety of Cavies.

Crested Guinea Pigs

These guinea pigs are extremely cute in appearance. They have extremely rounded and chubby bodies. They also have hair that is smooth and short. What is interesting to see is that there is a small swirl of white fur near the forehead. Usually, any guinea pig that has a certain color all over the body and just a swirl of differently colored hair on the forehead is called a crested guinea pig. Depending upon the color of the hair that is seen over the forehead, the breed is named. For instance, if the crest is white in color, it is called a white crested guinea pig.

Coronet Guinea Pig

The coronet guinea pig is an excellent combination of a silkie guinea pig and the crested guinea pig. The fur has really long strands of hair that are soft and extremely silky. In addition to that, there is a swirl of white or differently colored hair on the forehead of the animal.

Peruvian Guinea Pig

This is undoubtedly the most exotic variety of cavies available. It has the longest hair among all the guineas. The hair of these guineas falls over the eyes. There are also really long strands that fall down the back and the mid region of the rodent. They are available in a variety of colors and combinations. However, the only thing with this breed is that they are extremely difficult to maintain. They need a great deal of grooming and cleaning.

Silkie

The silkie is quite similar to the Peruvian breed. They also have very long strands of hair that fall down their body and their back. However, unlike the Peruvian guinea pig, they do not have long strands of hair on their face. Facial hair short and the features of the face can be seen distinctly. They are available in several colors and combinations.

Skinny Pig

This is the sphinx cat of guinea pigs. It may not appeal to everyone considering that it does not have the regular furry appearance that you expect with guinea pigs. They are almost hairless. They may have a few small strands of hair on their body. But, mostly they are hairless all over the body. You can see the wrinkles on their skin very distinctly. However, the best thing about this breed is that it is almost zero maintenance. You do not have to worry about messy fur or even matted areas on the fur.

Teddy Guinea Pig

As the name suggests, this guinea pig looks very similar to a teddy bear. It is extremely cute with fuzzy hair all over its body. The most adorable feature of this breed is that it can stand up just like a teddy bear. This breed is also available in a variety of combinations and can also be found in the satin variety.

Texel

This is perhaps the hardest to maintain breed among the cavies. It has long strands of hair on its coat. These strands are curly and need a lot of grooming to maintain well.

Once you have chosen the breed that you want to bring home, the next step is to ensure that you have a healthy pet as well. There are several factors like the place that you buy the guinea pig from and the conditions that the breeder has maintained them in that you need to consider along with the variety of guinea pig that you choose.

When you have a healthy and well-maintained pet, you can be assured that progressive care is also much easier and actually a lot of fun, too.

Guinea Pig Behavior

There are some distinct behavior patterns that you will observe with your guinea pigs. While most of it may seem normal, some behaviour patterns that are characteristic to guinea pigs may seem unnatural if you are not entirely aware of them. In fact, it is a lot of fun to watch guinea pigs in action. They can actually help you spend your entire day without a moment of boredom. They are rather edgy and active creatures that are sometimes quite funny as well. For the most part, guinea pigs are very calm, docile and gentle creatures and are a treat to have at home.

Here are some distinct guinea behaviour patterns that you will observe:

Aggression

Guinea pigs are rather docile and calm creatures. However, when threatened, they may show a bit of aggression as a mechanism for defence. The only thing that the guinea pigs will do is make a clacking sound with their teeth. They seldom direct this aggression towards their owners. But, when they do, it is best that you keep away. This behavior is most often exhibited when there are other guinea pigs in the cage and when they are fighting for their territory.

Begging for food

A guinea pig does not have to do much to gain the sympathy of his owner. Their cute and cuddly face is good enough to melt anyone's heart. However, guinea pigs may beg for food by making a scampering sound and may even go up on their hind limbs just like a dog. They become extremely excited and will look at you with great eagerness when they know that they could be in for a good veggie treat.

Barbering

This is not a very common behavior in guinea pigs. However, it is possible that they may indulge in it when they have cage mates. There is no understanding of why guinea pigs do this. However, there have been several instances when guinea pigs will chew the hair of their cage mates.

Biting

A guinea pig bites very seldom. Most often, they bite accidentally when they are actually going all out for a snack but get your finger instead. Guinea pigs also tend to bite or nibble at your clothes when you are holding them in your hands for a long time. This is their way of telling you that they need to relieve themselves and that they need to be put down immediately. Usually, guinea pigs do not soil their owner's garments. However, you can never be too sure. So, when you guinea pig begins to nibble it is in your best interest to put him down in his cage.

Biting Cage Bars

This behavior is quite typical of a guinea pig who is extremely bored. They tend to chew on the cage bars as an indication that they do not have enough to do. That may also mean that you are not giving your precious pet enough exercise time. Now, there is another reason why guinea pigs nibble at the cage bars. They may hear a sound that reminds them of their feeding time. Then, they do tend to get a tad bit excited and chew the bars in anticipation of the food that is to arrive.

Eating their Own Poop

I often thought of this as a rather disgusting behaviour. However, there is a scientific reason why these creatures practice this habit. The poop that guinea pigs eat is not the poop that you will see in the cage. This poop is consumed before it leaves the body and is small and soft in texture. This habit allows the guinea pig to reingest the food so that all the nutrients are completely absorbed. This is not possible in the first go as the digestive system of a cavy is too small to be able to do that.

Freezing

This is a behavior pattern that usually throws me into peals of laughter as it does any other guinea pig owner. The cavy will stand motionless for a few seconds and will become completely stiff. This behavior is depicted when the guinea pig is threatened by someone or something. Even when they hear a sudden loud noise, they may freeze as they are trying to take a moment to figure out how they can escape a certain situation. Sometimes, this freezing motion is followed by a vibrating sound of short intervals which indicates that the guinea pig is afraid.

Depression

If you notice that your guinea pig is sitting in a corner of the cage all day without responding even to his favourite treat, then you need to have your pet checked for a possible case of depression. They will show absolutely no interest in anything when they hit this phase. Sometimes they may be hiding some illness by staying quiet and aloof. This is a defence mechanism that they use in the wild so that the predators do not consider them vulnerable. It is important to ensure that your pet gets veterinary treatment immediately when they show any signs of depression.

Sniffing

If you introduce your guinea pig to another guinea pig, sniffing is a common behavior. The cavies tend to sniff the chin, nose and the bottom of the newly introduced companion. They may do this even when they are introduced to new people. Of course, they will not sniff your bottom but they will try to sniff the air around you to get more familiar with you.

Popcorning

This is a behavior pattern that is most often depicted by younger guinea pigs. They will walk around the cage and will suddenly jump up in the air. This is not practiced by the older guineas as they are heavier and cannot spring up with as much ease.

Hiding

In the initial days, there are chances that your guinea pig will not be as cuddly and friendly as your expect it to be. However, you must remember that the guinea pig is very low in the food chain. In addition to that, the defence options available to the animal are also limited. So, the guinea pig will most probably run away or hide from you for the first few days. There is no need to feel disheartened. When your guinea becomes familiar with your voice and scent, he should be able to get along with you just fine.

Scent Marking

When you have a male guinea pig in your home, you need to be prepared for scent marking. Guinea pigs will rub their bottom over a certain stretch of your home. That is their way of marking territory.

You need to be patient until you understand your guinea pig and vice versa. Just be gentle when you talk to your guinea pig. Make sure you spend enough time with your pet to make him feel reassured and comfortable in your presence.

Difference between a Guinea Pig and a Hamster

This is a rather important thing to know when you are deciding what rodent pet would be ideal for you. Hamsters and guinea pigs are very different from one another but are often mistaken for each other because of their similarity in appearance.

But, you need to know that a guinea pig is much larger than a hamster. It is also a lot calmer in nature. Hamsters, on the other hand, are active and smaller creatures. This is why you must NEVER encourage your pet guinea pig to exercise on a hamster wheel. This can lead to serious back and leg injuries to a guinea pig.

Hamsters are easily irritated and can nip when they feel annoyed. For this reason, they are most often kept in small cages all day long. A guinea pig, however, is more adaptable when it comes to being handled by people.

Guinea pigs are active all day long while hamsters are nocturnal creatures. If you bring home a hamster, you may see that he spends most of his time resting and sleeping. Guinea pigs are a lot more sociable and love being around people. Hamsters on the other hand are solitary and are not really looking for any company.

If you are looking for a companion, then you must bring home a guinea pig. These creatures can actually have long conversations with their owners, making their own distinct noises and sounds. A guinea pig does not need as many toys as a hamster as they are very happy being in the company of other guinea pigs or even their owners.

Whether you bring home a guinea pig or a hamster, you should know how to prepare your home for your pet. You must also be able to choose the right pet to bring home so that you do not have any rude surprises in the future. The next chapter deals with these essential preparation tips that will help you make your beloved pet feel more welcome. You will also know what to look for when you go guinea pig shopping.

Chapter 2: Cost of Owning a Guinea Pig

If you are planning to get home these cute little pets, then it would be sensible to have an idea of the initial and recurring costs that you are likely to incur. The initial cost of buying a guinea pig from a registered breeder will be somewhere around $ 30 - $ 40 depending on the exact breed and weight.

A typical breakdown of the allied costs of having the guinea pig at your home will be somewhat as under:

- Cage/ Housing: $50 (though is also a one-time investment)
- Pig Hay: $12 for a 40 Oz bag that will last about a month. The annual cost of hay will add up to $144 approximately.
- Bedding: Good quality paper bedding of large size will be about $ 20 a piece which will last about a month. So this element itself will add up $ 240 to the annual cost.
- Dry Pellet: It costs $15 for a 5 Lb bag and you will need about 3 bags a year making the total cost of pellets to be around $ 45.
- Fruit and vegetable snacks: You could safely count for about $20 per month making the annual expenditure about $240 depending on the exact variety that you provide you guinea pigs with.
- Vet care: On an average $50 per year will be required for veterinary care per guinea pig (annual checkup).

All the above-listed factors will imply that the average cost of maintaining one guinea pig at your home will somewhere between $600 to $800 per year. Having understood the cost factor, you will now be in a much better position to take the next step in understanding what goes into selecting, buying and keeping guinea pigs as pets.

Chapter 3: Bringing Home a Guinea Pig

Bringing a guinea pig home is not as easy as going out, picking a cute looking rodent and putting it in a cage. You need to make sure that your home is prepared to have a pet that is as docile and delicate as a guinea pig. There are several things that can go wrong, proving to be fatal to your pet sometimes. So, the entire family must be in sync with the preps that you make when you bring home your guinea pig or just about any pet for that matter.

Choosing a Guinea Pig

It is always recommended you use caution when buying guinea pigs from pet stores. These stores sometimes bring in the animals from mills where they kept in very unhealthy conditions. This means that the guinea pigs could be sickly and could be carrying several diseases. Even show breeders are not entirely reliable unless they are recommended to you by someone you know. Most breeders pay very little attention to the temperament and the health of the breeds that they produce. The best option is to look for guinea pig adoption homes or even exotic rescue shelters when you plan to bring home a guinea pig.

You could either ask for recommendations, or you could visit several websites that are available. Be sure to check for the reviews and ratings of websites before you make any buying commitments. If you are unsatisfied with the websites that you have found, you could also look up your local telephone directory to get some leads. When you have found a reliable source to buy your guinea pigs from, there are a couple of guidelines and tips that you must adhere to before you give the final nod for a particular piglet.

The next step is to ensure that your guinea pig is completely healthy. Here are a few guidelines to check the health of your guinea pig:

- Take a good look at the body condition of the guinea pig. The animal should neither be too skinny or too fat. There should not be any lumps, bumps or swellings on the body of the animal when you are examining it.
- The attitude of your guinea pig is of great importance. These creatures are usually very bright and curious. On the other hand, if they are lethargic, then you need to be worried.
- The coat should always be well groomed. The signs of a good coat include smooth, full and fluffy fur all over the body. There should be absolutely no bald patches on the body of your guinea pig. Another thing that you need to avoid is a guinea pig that may have any red patches on the skin. When you are examining the fur, look out for extensive soiling in the rear end of the body. This could be an indication of diarrhoea. It could also mean that the guinea pig has not been kept under clean and healthy conditions.
- There should be no discharge near the eyes, ears or the nose. If this happens, it could be a sign of some form of infection that the rodent is suffering from. You must check the fur around these areas to see if there are any crusts, stains or any sign of wetness.
- The teeth are an important indication of good health in most animals. With the guinea pigs, you need to ensure that the teeth are not too large or overgrown. The

alignment should also be clean and neat. The next thing you need to do is check for any signs of wetness or matted fur on the chin area.

- The breathing of the guinea pig should be closely observed. If you see that the breathing is labored with a distinct clicking or gurgling sound, you need to be alert to it. The typical breathing pattern for a guinea pig is quiet and even.
- The next step is to watch how the guinea pig moves. There should be no signs of straining or lameness in the movements. In addition to that, any stiffness or reluctance to move could be a sign of some muscular or orthopaedic condition that the guinea pig is suffering from.
- You must also make sure that you check the surroundings of the guinea pig thoroughly. The cage that the guinea pig is housed in must be clean. The access to water and food should be easy. If the cage is too overcrowded, then there are chances that a guinea pig may develop some diseases when it comes in contact with another one that is carrying a certain disease. The conditions under which the guinea pig is maintained should ensure that there is absolutely no stress caused to the animal under any circumstance.
- The behaviour of the guinea pig is the next thing that you must check. Watch how the guinea pig reacts to people. Usually, they may squirm a little and be skittish in the beginning. However, a guinea pig is very easily adaptable to human touch. The animal must not overly resist being handled and touched. The next thing is that the guinea pig should be alert and active. Even if they are willing to come to you, they should be slightly curious. The animal should sniff around and try to familiarise itself with you. On the other hand, a lethargic guinea pig may be extremely easy

to handle. However, you will see a distinct lack of interest in the demeanour of the animal.

-
- Make sure you follow all these steps of checking the health of your new pet to be. This entire examination process will take you exactly ten minutes to complete. Of course, if you are buying a guinea pig from a breeder, they should be able to provide you with a health certificate or a breed certificate. On the other hand, when you approach a rescue shelter, be prepared for animals with behavioural problems or signs of abuse.
-
-

Guinea pig Buying Tips

-
- Here are some tips that will help you look at other aspects of the guinea pig besides its health. You can make a checklist if you are a first-time pet owner to ensure that you follow all the health guidelines and tips to bring home the ideal pet.
-
- Check the age of the guinea pig. Ideally, it is a good idea to bring home the youngest piglet available with the breeder or the shelter. The right age to bring home a guinea pig is when it is about 6 weeks old or slightly older.
- Even if the guinea pig that you choose looks extremely healthy, make sure you check the pigs that it is sharing its cage with. If you feel like a guinea pig has companions or cage mates that are not exactly very healthy, you can avoid adopting from a particular shelter or breeder. There are chances that the illness that you notice in the other guinea pigs is contagious. So, if you have other pets or even guinea pigs at home, you risk the spreading of

infections. Also, the longevity of a guinea pig is compromised when he is maintained under unhealthy conditions.
- The breeder should have kept the males and the females separately. When you are bringing home a guinea pig, be extremely sure to check the gender of your guinea pig. If you are getting a female that is over 6 weeks old, you must ensure that she is not pregnant. The worst thing that you have to deal with is unexpected litters when you are just getting used to the idea of having a guinea pig in your home. In fact, guinea pigs as young as 4 weeks old could be pregnant. So, make sure you check thoroughly.
-
- You may want to choose a shelter to get your guinea pig from. There is an adoption network dedicated to guinea pigs. These rescue homes can introduce you to guinea pigs that need a new home and a well-deserved second chance.
-
- However, if you are insistent on buying a guinea pig from a breeder, you should make sure that you are familiar with the breeding goals of the breeder. They should have some temperament and health goals that will make your guinea a good pet to bring home.

Chapter 4: Guinea Pig Care

Once you have picked the ideal pet and brought it home, the next step is to ensure that you are able to provide good conditions for the rodent to thrive in. Housing is the first thing you need to worry about if you have other pets at home. These creatures are very low in the food chain and have very little ability to protect themselves. So, make sure that you first build a nice home for your guinea pig.

Housing for Guinea Pigs

You may either choose a cage or a guinea pig hutch to house your guinea pigs. Irrespective of what you choose, the preparation that is required is more or less the same. You need to make sure that the housing that you choose for your guinea pig is comfortable and safe. The ideal size of the cage for guinea pigs is as follow:

- 1 Guinea Pig: Minimum 7.5 sq.ft but preferred is 30" x 36"
- 2 Guinea Pigs: Minimum 7.5 sq.ft but preferred is 30' x 50"
- 3 Guinea Pigs: Minimum 10.5 sq.ft but preferred is 30 x 76"

The site

The first step is to choose the right spot to place the guinea pig housing. You need to make sure that your precious pet is well protected from rain, wind, direct sunlight and heat. Any of these elements in excess can affect the health and well-being of your guinea pig.

Though some vets will recommend keeping the guinea pigs outside too, but extreme care must be taken to ensure that your pets are not exposed to direct sunlight or excessive humidity. Additionally places that experience outside temperatures below 18 degrees or above 24 degrees are not suitable for the cage being placed in the open.

In case you choose to place the shelter outdoor, make sure that it is on a surface that is levelled. Never place the guinea pig cage on the edge of a table or a rack in the garden as there is the risk of the cage or hutch toppling over. You need to make sure that your roof of the hutch is completely waterproof. There should be no direct sunlight or rain in the area that you have chosen to place the guinea pig housing.

When you keep the shelter indoors, you need to ensure that the temperature of the room is maintained at a constant. If there are any drafts that could creep into the room, have the areas shut off. You also need to make sure that the heating and cooling systems are moderated. There should be no source of direct sunlight or heat in the room that you have chosen for your guinea pig housing.

Preparing the housing

It is best to prepare the housing of the guinea pig well before you actually go and pick a guinea pig to bring home. That way, you will have a shelter that is ready and waiting for your pet when you bring him home.

The first thing you need to do in order to prepare your hutch or cage is to make the floor of the housing. That means you need to have a thick layer of hay or wood shavings across the floor of the housing that you have chosen. That way the floor will be protected from the droppings and the urine of the guinea pig. If you do not have enough absorbent material for your guinea pig, there are chances that he will develop some infection because of the unhygienic conditions of the cage.

You also need an additional layer of thick hay in one corner of the hutch. This is where your guinea pig will rest and feed. Usually, the enclosed end of the housing that you choose is used for this bed or nesting area for your guinea pig.

Then, you need to make sure that food is readily available to your pet. Place a small bowl or food dish filled with pellets or veggies for your new pet. You need to make sure that the housing area is large enough to hold the guinea pig and his food. This prevents any spilling or soiling.

On one side of the hutch you need to fasten a water bottle. The bottle should be at a height that is convenient for the guinea pig to reach up to. Fill this bottle up and check for proper water flow. You can use your finger to check if the water flow is continuous. In case it is not allowing water to pass through easily, you can squeeze the bottle gently.

The primary concern with cage preparation is to ensure that there is enough food, water, littering space and also resting space for your furry little friend.

Adding toys

You may also add several toys to the hutch or cage. The toys are usually the ones that your guinea pig can chew or push around with his nose. Ideal toys for guinea pigs are edible logs, thisle houses, hideaway huts etc. Various designs of tunnels are also considered handy for keeping the life of a guinea pig interesting and action packed. Never give him a hamster wheel as he is not built to run like a hamster. The regular guinea pig toys can mentally stimulate your pet and make sure that he gets enough exercise all day long. When you place toys in the housing area, make sure that they are large enough for your pet not to swallow. Also, the cage or hutch should not be too small and cluttered with toys.

There are other accessories like a salad rack or a hay rack that you can get from local pet stores. If your cage or hutch is large enough, make sure you include them in the right place.

Maintaining the housing area

The guinea pig hutch or cage needs to be well maintained to prevent any infection. You need to clean the hutch out on a regular basis. This has to be done very meticulously in order to save time and also not trouble the little furry inhabitant.

You must make sure that the hutch is cleaned every week at least. You must remove the guinea pigs from the hutch and take the entire floor covering out. This is where all the mess is soaked in and absorbed. Once that is taken care of, remove the left over veggies and guinea pig food. You also need to empty the water bottle out and wash it thoroughly.

You may choose to wash the entire hutch or wipe it down with organic cleaners. Make sure you do not use to many chemicals to clean the hutch as it may affect the health of your guinea pig. Then, just replace all these contents with new ones and your guinea pig is good to go back into his favourite hideout.

Feeding your Guinea Pigs

When it comes to feeding a guinea pig, you need to be prepared for the fact that these creatures are extremely messy eaters. They tend to mess up their food bowls and also their water bowls. This is why it is recommended that you have water given to them through a bottle on the side of their hutch or cage. That way, it is less messy.

It is not common for guinea pigs to overeat. However, you need to keep a tab on the foods that you give them throughout the day. Even a little bit of imbalance in their diet can lead to serious health issues. There are three feeding options for guinea pigs. You can give them commercial food, hay and vegetables. Of course, fruits work, too. What you need to remember is the proportion of the foods that you give your cavies. When you find the right balance, you can optimise nutrition for your little ones.

Commercial food: You can give your guinea pig about 1/8 cup of commercially made pellets each day. When you are giving them dry foods like pellets, make sure you supplement it with ample fruits and vegetables. You also need to provide your guinea pigs with enough water when they are consuming dry pellets.

Commercially available dry pellets are composed of vitamin supplements, soybean meals,calcium carbonate, calcium phosphate, alfalfa meal, wheat middlings, salt, ground corn, ferrous and copper sulphates, magnesium oxide, sodium selenite,cobalt carbonate and riboflavin supplements etc.

Hay: Special timothy hay is available for guinea pigs. Make sure that there is a good supply of this hay available for your guinea pig as it aids digestion. Another important function of timothy hay is that it keeps the growth of a guinea pig's teeth controlled. Else, the teeth can be really sharp and can cause damage around the hutch and even your home.

Fruits and veggies: Now, these are a cavy's favourite foods. You must ensure that the guinea pigs get fresh fruits and vegetables at least once every day. One cup of leafy greens like lettuce, parsley and spinach should be good enough for a cavy each day. Twice a week, you can add foods like sweet potato, carrots and zucchini to the food bowl.

Cavies also love fruits. They can be given once a day. The portion of fruit given to a cavy must be controlled as the sugar levels in fruits are high. A wedge of orange or apple or a few blueberries should be good enough for a guinea pig each day.

There are several commercial treats that you can buy for your guinea pig. Of course, it is best to limit these treats to the training sessions. Instead, you could give your cavy fruits and veggies as a treat. The commercial ones have very little nutritional value and will not do much to keep the good health of your beloved pet.

In addition to this, commercially available treats can be really expensive. The guinea pigs will love fruits or leafy greens as treats if they are never introduced to these commercial treats. If you want to make your pet a fun snack, you can try to add some rolled oats to the pellets that you are feeding your guinea pig.

Mineral wheels: You can buy multivitamin wheels or mineral wheels from the market. These wheels can supplement your guinea pig's diet. They also act as an outlet for the chewing needs of your furry pals. Of course, if your guinea pig is eating a well-balanced meal every day, there will be little or no need for such mineral wheels.

The only concern with these wheels is the glue or the adhesive that holds them together. They could cause a lot of harm to your pet. In addition to that, the manufacturing process of these wheels involves a lot of chemicals that should not be a part of your guinea's diet. Unless your vet recommends a mineral wheel, it is a good idea to give your pet a good meal each day and nothing additional.

Serving the food

Instead of giving your guinea pig a plastic serving bowl, opt for a ceramic one. The latter is sturdier and is resistant to all the chewing that will most certainly ensue when you have a guinea pig. They will not crack or chip easily and are hence a lot more durable.

A wide and shallow bowl is ideal for a guinea pig. Most guineas like to place their front feet on the rim of the container that they eat from. If you have a shallow bowl, the chances of it tipping over are fewer.

The food should be placed far away from the litter area. Then, you need to keep spot cleaning your guinea pig's feeding bowl each week. You must check if there is any bedding material or droppings in the food bowl. You can wash the food bowl with soapy water on a weekly basis. Then, allow it to dry thoroughly. This is a healthy practice that you can make a part of the routine cleaning that you will be doing each week. That way, you can ensure that the eating conditions of your cavy are hygienic.

You need to also make sure that the food is always fresh. When you are providing your guinea pig with produce each day, you need to get rid of any uneaten food bits. This includes fruits and vegetables that may spoil if they are left uneaten for long hours. You need to check if the guinea pig has eaten all the fruits and veggies an hour after serving them. As for the dry pellets, you can replace them each day.

If you see that there is too much produce or pellets left over each day, this is a sign that you are giving your guinea pig too much food.

Veterinary Care for Guinea Pigs

The good news about guinea pigs is that they do not require any shots like your dog or your cat. However, they definitely need to have a good vet who can attend to them when they are unwell. You must remember that no matter what pet you have, the vet can play a significant role in its care. There may be several medical emergencies when you need to go looking for a vet. So, it is a good idea to make a note of a reliable vet in your area to take your little pet to.

The vets who usually attend to pets like cats and dogs are not qualified to take care of guinea pigs. For these pets, you need to look for someone who specialises in exotic pets. Even if a vet tells you that he or she can attend to your cavy, do not be fooled. You need someone who has experience with guinea pigs. A general vet will come in handy in case of a serious emergency.

Make sure that you take your cavy for wellness checks every six months. You may also opt for an annual check-up which should work just fine with your cavy. Pet insurance is an option available to make your veterinary visits less expensive. Of course, you can get this insurance from your vet or can look up the internet for reliable sources and leads.

Remember that neutering and spaying are not necessary for a cavy. They will not have any behavioural changes with a guinea pig as they do with dogs and cats. It is only recommended that you neuter a guinea pig when you are going to place them in a cage with other females. So, if you plan to take your cavy to the vet for neutering, make sure that you take as many precautions as you can to ensure that your cavy is in good health after the procedure. Only go to a vet who has enough experience with neutering cavies. He should have had a high success rate while performing the surgery as well.

Training a Guinea Pig

Guinea pigs are extremely friendly and sociable creatures. They can adapt to human company quite easily and will respond to your commands and your cues if you are a little patient and are willing to spend some time with the cavy. All you need is a handful of treats, and a great deal of patience, and you should be successful in teaching your guinea pig the following tricks:

Come when called: You can teach the guinea pig to come to you when you call out his name. For this, all you need to do is say his name and then give him a treat. Repeat this for several days or even several times each day until you notice that the guinea looks at you when you call his name even before you give him a treat. Then, you will move on to saying his name and unfolding the treat on your palm a few inches away and then wait for him to come to you. You can inch away from your pet as he gets familiar with the concept that coming to you when called will earn him a treat. Then you can just call out to him and he will come to you. Remember, you need to give your guinea pig a treat when he responds to being called to come. If you do not do this, he may just forget the entire training, and you will have to start from scratch all over.

Sit up and beg: This is a trait that guinea pigs naturally exhibit. They are able to go up on their hind legs just like cats or dogs. However, the challenge is to get them to do this on your command. Hold a treat above your guinea pig's head and allow him to sit up to beg for the food. When he does this, give him the treat. Now, add a verbal command or gesture to this and whenever he responds correctly to it, give him a treat. Eventually, your guinea pig will learn to sit up on command, expecting a treat, of course.

Litter box training: This type of training is not reserved for cats and dogs. Even pets like guinea pigs can be trained to use the litter box. However, they may not follow this as diligently as the other pets. You can place the litter box in a spot in the cage where the guinea pig often goes to relieve himself. Now, put some hay in this box and also add a few fecal pellets in it. If the guinea pig uses this litter box, give him a treat as a token of your appreciation. He may make mistakes when he is being trained. However, you need to ignore this and give him a treat only when he successfully follows the practice of using a litter box. Remember, that they guinea pig may or may not use the litter box as it is not exactly natural behaviour for them.

When you are training your guinea pig, try to be gentle and sweet. They can get intimidated by an authoritative voice. Use a treat that your guinea loves the best. This should be the special treat that you give your cavy when he exhibits behaviour that you want him to.

If he makes a mistake, simply ignore it. They are going to get a few things wrong in the process. However, you must never scold or punish a guinea pig. They will most likely just get frightened of you and will stop interacting with you altogether.

Instead use positive reinforcements and be appreciative when your guinea does something you want him to. That will encourage them to spend more time with you and be responsive to what you are telling them to do. When you get the hang of training the guinea pig for these basic commands, you can try more complex skills that can be used in shows as well.

Showing a guinea pig can be loads of fun. Of course, it does require a good amount of preparation as well. You need to make sure that your guinea pig is ready for a show. The next chapter talks in detail about showing your guinea pig and grooming him for a show as well.

Chapter 5: Showing a Guinea Pig

It is always fun to show your pet off. With guinea pigs as well, there are specially designed shows that you can enrol for. Your guinea pig will be judged on the basis of his appearance and skills. However, that aside, showing is a great opportunity to bond with your pet.

Introduction to showing guinea pigs

Guinea pig shows are usually attended by guinea pig fanciers who are mostly into breeding and showing the animal. There are two main groups for showing your guinea pig.

The first group is the purebred section. This is for certain recognised guinea pig breeds such as the Abyssinian. There are several long haired varieties that are also showcased for this division. There are several standards and guidelines that are recommended for these purebred guinea pigs. There are special clubs dedicated to each pure breed where you can find several pictures and also records of animals that have been recognised for outstanding performance.

The next category is the pets. These pigs are not of a certain breed. They may just be a mixture of various pet breeds and are usually cross breeds. In these cases, the judges are not looking for certain standards or characteristics. Instead, they are judged on the basis of how clean they are and how social they are.

There are several pet classes that you can take your guinea pig to when you decide to show him. You need to keep three important things in mind to ensure that your pet is successful in his classes.

- He should be bathed and cleaned regularly. The coat should be free from spots, matting, grease, etc. He should not have any loose hair if he is of the long haired variety.
- The guinea pig should be healthy. The physical condition of the guinea pig must be up to the mark. The pig should not be fat. Instead, he should look fit, muscular and should have bright eyes and a shiny coat.
- Your guinea pig should be used to people. If he does not like being handled, he may not be calm when placed on a judging table. If the pig is younger, he could be a little skiddish - that is allowed. However, as the guinea pig grows older and has more show experience, he is expected to be calmer.
-
- There are several shows that are conducted on a local or national level. You can choose the show that you want to attend and register yourself and your pet. There may be a small fee attached to the registration. After you have enrolled, you have nothing else to do but groom your pet and have a great time at the show.
-

Grooming a Guinea Pig

Grooming a guinea pig just before a show is an absolute must. If your pig looks shabby and unkempt, he will stand no chance of being appreciated at a show. There are some grooming processes that you can follow. Make a checklist and ensure you have everything in place just before you present your guinea pig to the world:

- **Bathe:** You must give your guinea pig a bath at least one week before a show when he has short hair. However, you must bathe him two weeks prior to the show if he has long hair. When you give your guinea pig a bath, his fur will get a nice shine as the natural oils that are secreted by the skin are stimulated. There are specially designed shampoos for guinea pigs and smaller pets. Make sure you use a recommended shampoo only. You can bath him in a sink with some warm water.
-
- **Flea dip:** After you have given your guinea pig a good bath, the next step is to give him a good dip in some flea dip product. This should be done at least a week before the show to make sure that there are no lice or lice eggs on the fur and skin. You may consult your veterinarian to recommend some dip products and the right way to use these products on your cavy. Make sure that you follow the steps provided by your vet to keep your cavy safe.
-
- **Clip:** The nails of a guinea pig have to be clipped on a regular basis. Make sure that you have one session of nail clipping just before a show. This prevents the nail from curling up and looking rather hideous. When nails grow too long, they can also prick into the paws of your guinea pig and eventually cause infections. The nails should always be neat and short. If you are clipping guinea pig nails for the first time, make sure you take him to a vet. If you do it wrong, you could injure the delicate paws of the animal. When you clip the nails regularly, your pig will also become used to this process and will be at ease every time you decide to give his nails a clip.

- **Degrease:** There are certain grease glands that are present on the rump of the animal's body where they would normally have a tail. Male cavies, in particular, tend to secrete a certain sticky substance and a particular scent from this region when they reach sexual maturity. When you are about to show the animal, you must make sure that any built up grease is removed from the area. You can use a simple cotton ball and some eucalyptus oil to get rid of any excess grease on the body.

- Once you have done all of the above, all you need to do is style your cavy. If your cavy has long hair, make sure you brush it well just before the show. Pay special attention to the body and the back of the animal as there are chances of soiling and matting due to feces or urine. Of course, you can add that pretty little bow or accessories to make your cavy look a lot more adorable.

Chapter 6: Pregnancy and Birth

To begin with you have to understand that it is not recommended to have your guinea pigs mate. In many situations, such mating can prove fatal to female guinea pig if not cared for properly.

However, if you have a female and male cavy together, you may have to deal with pregnant cavies as well. Most pet owners choose to have their pets neutered before they reach the age of sexual maturity. Typically, for a guinea pig this happens when they are between 6 weeks to 10 weeks of age. You need to be able to take good care of a cavy when she is pregnant. Of course, you don't have to do much besides making sure that you keep her well fed and comfortable.

Mating Behavior

Guinea pigs indulge in a special mating dance when they are ready to mate. They tend to shake their hips from side to side and try to show the ladies some moves. Then they make a certain vibrating sound which is called 'motorboating'.

The most dominant male in a group is the first one to mount a female. This is normal behaviour. There are also chances that females mount each other when they are in heat. However, when males mount one another, it is a sign of aggression.

The mounting lasts for a couple of seconds and may take place a few times in an hour. This is the only time when you can see evidently aggressive behaviour among guinea pigs that are otherwise quite calm and docile.

Pregnancy

The gestation period for a cavy is about 72 days. The pregnancy is shorter when the mother is carrying more babies. The pregnancy is very easy and is usually with no problems at all. The only thing you need to be concerned about is maintaining the right temperature. It must be a cool environment for your pregnant guinea pig to thrive in. There have been several cases of death due to heat in the later pregnancy stages.

When you are handling a pregnant guinea pig, make sure that you support her hind quarters and lift her up without any jerk. In the first four weeks, you will see no evident behavioural changes in the cavy. In the last three weeks, the pregnant cavy will become extremely plump. This is when the babies make up close to half the body weight of the mother.

Make sure you give your cavy enough calcium. You can feed her alfalfa hay instead of the regular timothy hay that you give her. In addition to this, you can also give her foods that are high in fiber. This prevents a common occurrence during pregnancy which is hair thinning. To prevent any toxaemia, you need to double up the vitamin C that you are providing your cavy. You can ask your vet for supplements and medicines that you need for your cavy to have a comfortable delivery with healthy babies.

The Babies

It is only with the first pregnancy that your guinea pig will require some assistance. After that, they will manage the whole process pretty much on their own. The hip bones of the guinea pig tend to grow closer as they grow until they become pregnant. So, if you have a guinea pig that is over six weeks of age and is in her first pregnancy, you need to take assistance from your vet. You need to make sure that your guinea pig will be able to have a normal delivery. If your vet recommends a caesarean, you must opt for it as it may save your guinea pig's life.

The first sign of the upcoming birth is that the babies will move around in the womb. The actual birth of the babies is a very simple affair. It will take place during the day and will be done in about 20 minutes. After about 5 minutes of labor, the first baby will emerge. Usually, a guinea pig will have about 3 babies at a time. Sometimes, there are more, too. You need to become alert if the labor lasts for too long. This is when she needs to be rushed to the vet, failing which she could succumb to exhaustion.

When the babies are born, they will come out head first. After this, the mother will pull the amniotic sac with her teeth. She will then clean the babies. The last thing that your cavy will do is consume the placenta as a source of nutrition.

To avoid any mishap, it is a good idea to separate a cavy from the others after birth. All you need to provide is some extra soft nesting and bedding. Also, make sure that there is enough food and water for the new mother.

Conclusion

Thank you for reading this book. You should now enough information about guinea pigs by now to decide if it is the right pet for you or not & the basics of guinea pig care. Here are some things that you need to keep in mind when you bring home a guinea pig:

- Make sure you are ready for the financial commitment. A guinea pig may cost you between $35-65 per month for just the basics.
- Make time for your pet. Guinea pigs tend to become depressed and lonely when they do not have enough companionship.
- Keep larger pets away. Guinea pigs are easily threatened and may develop illnesses or behavioural problems when they are threatened by other pets in your house.
- Maintain hygiene standards. Although guinea pigs carry diseases seldom, it is a good idea to have children, and other members of your family wash their hands after handling the pet. The cleaner you keep your guinea pig the safer it is.

I hope that this book has answered all your questions about the guinea pig. If you have decided to bring one home, then I would like to congratulate you on the years of happiness that you have just invested in.

Printed in Great Britain
by Amazon